*For Waldo*

This edition published 1993
First published in Great Britain by Walker Books Ltd

Library of Congress Cataloging in Publication Data
Handford, Martin
Where's Waldo?
Summary: The reader follows Waldo as he hikes around the world and must try
to find him in the illustrations of some of the crowded places he visits.
1. Literary recreations   [1. Literary recreations]
2. Voyages and travels—fiction.   3. Humorous stories]   1. Title
PZ7.H1918Wh   1987   [Fic]   87-2606
ISBN 0-316-34391-9

10  9  8  7  6  5  4  3  2  1

Printed and bound by L.E.G.O., Vicenza, Italy

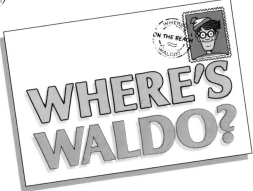

# WHERE'S WALDO?

# MARTIN HANDFORD

HI, FRIENDS!

MY NAME IS WALDO.
I'M JUST SETTING OFF ON A WORLDWIDE
HIKE. YOU CAN COME TOO. ALL YOU HAVE
TO DO IS FIND ME, WHEREVER I GO.

I'VE GOT ALL I NEED – WALKING STICK,
KETTLE, MALLET, CUP, BACKPACK, SLEEPING
BAG, BINOCULARS, CAMERA, SNORKEL, BELT,
BAG AND SHOVEL.

BY THE WAY, I'M NOT TRAVELING ON MY
OWN. THAT'S MY DOG, WOOF, AND WENDA
BEHIND ME, AND TEN WALDO-WATCHERS.
WHEREVER I GO, WOOF AND WENDA ARE
THERE SOMEWHERE – THOUGH ALL YOU CAN
EVER SEE OF WOOF IS HIS TAIL. WATCH OUT
FOR THE WALDO-WATCHERS TOO – EACH
APPEARS ONCE ON MY TRAVELS.

FIND ALL OF US, IF YOU CAN.

Waldo

GREETINGS,
WALDO FOLLOWERS!
WOW, THE BEACH WAS
GREAT TODAY! I SAW
THIS GIRL STICK AN
ICE CREAM IN HER
BROTHER'S FACE, AND
THERE WAS A SAND
CASTLE WITH A REAL
KNIGHT IN ARMOUR
INSIDE! FANTASTIC!

Waldo

TO:
WALDO FOLLOWERS,
HERE, THERE,
EVERYWHERE.

WHERE'S
ON THE BEACH
WALDO

YODEL-ODEL-EE,
WALDO'S GANG!
I WALKED ACROSS THE SKI
SLOPES TODAY AND SAW
SOME _INCREDIBLE_ SIGHTS!
THERE WAS THIS SKIER
GIVING FLOWERS TO HIS
GIRLFRIEND, AND ANOTHER
WITH AN ANCHOR OVER HIS
SHOULDER, AND ONE ALL
ROLLED UP IN A SNOWBALL!
WOW! INCREDIBLE!
KEEP LOOKING FOR ME!

Waldo

TO:
WALDO'S GANG,
UPSTAIRS,
DOWNSTAIRS,
ALL OVER THE PLACE.

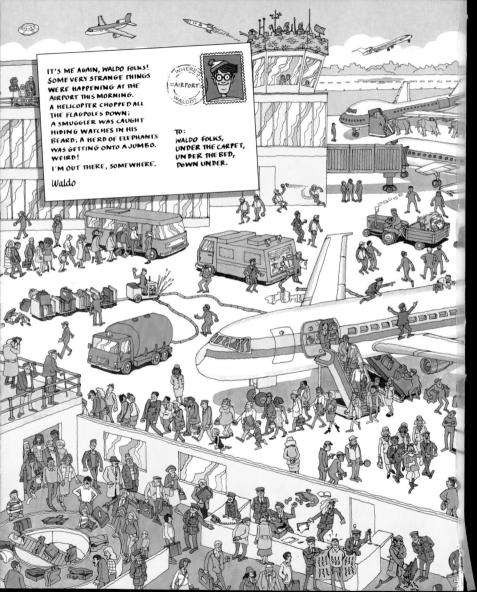

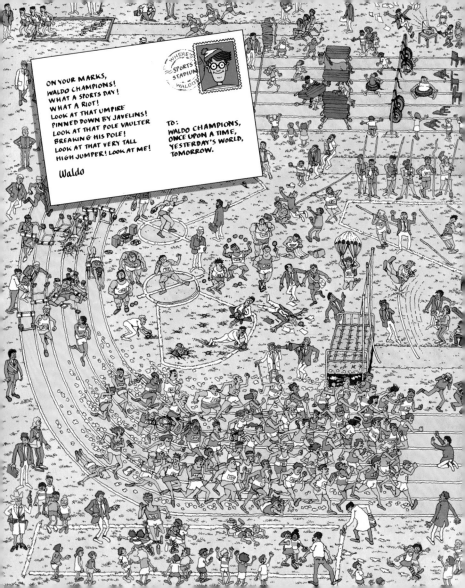

ON YOUR MARKS,
WALDO CHAMPIONS!
WHAT A SPORTS DAY!
WHAT A RIOT!
LOOK AT THAT UMPIRE
PINNED DOWN BY JAVELINS!
LOOK AT THAT POLE VAULTER
BREAKING HIS POLE!
LOOK AT THAT VERY TALL
HIGH JUMPER! LOOK AT ME!

Waldo

TO:
WALDO CHAMPIONS,
ONCE UPON A TIME,
YESTERDAY'S WORLD,
TOMORROW.

HOW-DE-DOO, WALDO SCHOLARS!
I'M CLEVER, AS YOU KNOW.
I GO TO MUSEUMS TO LEARN
THINGS. TODAY I FOUND OUT
ABOUT TICKLING THE TOES OF
A MAN IN THE STOCKS; ABOUT
KNOCKING DOWN A SUIT OF
ARMOUR; ABOUT THE
EGYPTIAN MUMMY'S BABY.
NOW THAT'S LEARNING!
HAVE YOU LEARNED TO FIND ME?

*Waldo*

TO:
WALDO SCHOLARS,
AT SCHOOL,
IN TROUBLE,
AGAIN.

ANCHORS AWAY, WALDO MATES!
WELL, SUCH WONDERS I SAW
AT SEA, AHOY, AHOY! A LOBSTER
ON A FLOATING BED! A CAPSIZED
DESERT ISLAND! A SHARK IN
A SWIMMING POOL! THE ONLY
QUESTION IS, CAN YOU SEA ME?
HA-HA!

Waldo

TO:
WALDO MATES,
DOWN THE PLUGHOLE,
UP THE CREEK.

WATCH IT, WALDO HUNTERS!
I'M AN ANIMAL LOVER, THAT'S
FOR SURE. I LOVE THAT HIPPO
WITH ITS ALARM CLOCK; THAT
LION HAVING ITS MANE COMBED;
THE HAT-EATING GIRAFFE; THE
OWLS IN SPECTACLES. GREAT!
.NOW TRACK ME DOWN, IF YOU
DARE.

Waldo

TO:
WALDO HUNTERS,
NICE PLACE,
THE JUNGLE,
OUTSIDE.

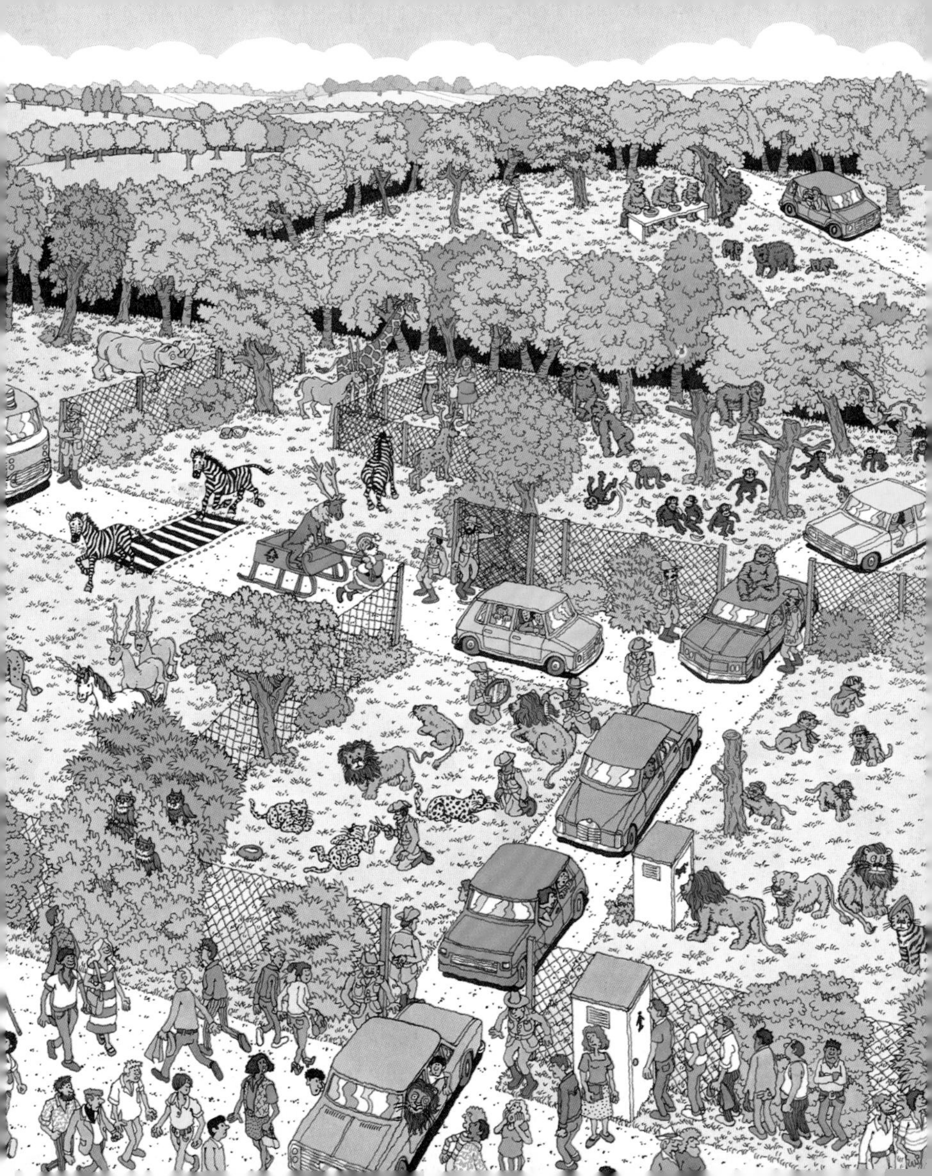

WOTCHA, WALDO WATCHERS!
SAW SOME TRULY TERRIFIC
SIGHTS TODAY - SOMEONE
BURNING TROUSERS WITH
AN IRON; A LONG THIN MAN
WITH A LONG THIN TIE;
A GLOVE ATTACKING A MAN.
PHEW! INCREDIBLE!

Waldo

TO:
WALDO WATCHERS,
OVER THE MOON,
THE WILD WEST,
NOW.

ROLL UP, WALDO FUN LOVERS! WOW, I'VE LOST ALL MY THINGS, ONE IN EVERY PLACE. NOW YOU HAVE TO GO BACK AND FIND THEM. AND WENDA LOST HER UMBRELLA SOMEWHERE – CAN ANYBODY FIND IT? WORST OF ALL, THE BOBBLE'S MISSING FROM ONE WALDO-WATCHER'S HAT – WHICH HAT, AND WHERE IS THE BOBBLE?

Waldo

WHERE FAIRGROUND WALDO?

# THE GREAT WHERE'S WALDO? CHECKLIST
Hundreds more things for Waldo watchers to watch out for!

## IN TOWN
- [ ] A dog on a roof
- [ ] A man on a fountain
- [ ] A man about to trip over a dog's leash
- [ ] A car crash
- [ ] A keen barber
- [ ] People in a street, watching TV
- [ ] A puncture caused by a Roman arrow
- [ ] A tearful tune
- [ ] A boy attacked by a plant
- [ ] A waiter who isn't concentrating
- [ ] A robber who's been clobbered
- [ ] A face on a wall
- [ ] A man coming out of a manhole
- [ ] A man feeding pigeons
- [ ] A bicycle crash

## THE RAILWAY STATION
- [ ] A boy falling from a train
- [ ] A breakdown on tracks
- [ ] Naughty children on a train roof
- [ ] People being knocked over by a door
- [ ] A man about to step on a ball
- [ ] Three different times at the same time
- [ ] A wheelbarrow baby carriage
- [ ] A face on a train
- [ ] Five people reading one newspaper
- [ ] A struggling bag carrier
- [ ] A show-off with suitcases
- [ ] A man losing everything from his cases
- [ ] A smoking train
- [ ] A squeeze on a bench
- [ ] A dog tearing a man's trousers
- [ ] Fare dodgers
- [ ] A hand caught between doors
- [ ] A cattle stampede
- [ ] A man breaking a weighing machine

## SKI SLOPES
- [ ] A man reading on a roof
- [ ] A flying skier
- [ ] A runaway skier
- [ ] A backward skier
- [ ] A portrait in snow
- [ ] An illegal fisherman
- [ ] A snowball in the neck
- [ ] Two unconscious skiers
- [ ] Two skiers hitting trees
- [ ] An Alpine horn
- [ ] A snow skier
- [ ] A flag collector
- [ ] Two very scruffy skiers
- [ ] A skier up a tree
- [ ] A water skier on snow
- [ ] A Yeti
- [ ] A skiing reindeer
- [ ] A roof jumper
- [ ] A heap of skaters

## ON THE BEACH
- [ ] A dog biting a boy's bottom
- [ ] A man who is overdressed
- [ ] A muscular man with a medal
- [ ] A popular girl
- [ ] A water skier on water
- [ ] A striped photo
- [ ] A punctured pontoon
- [ ] A donkey who likes ice cream
- [ ] A man being squashed
- [ ] A punctured beach ball
- [ ] A human pyramid
- [ ] A human stepping-stone
- [ ] Two odd friends
- [ ] A cowboy
- [ ] A human donkey
- [ ] Age and beauty
- [ ] A boy who follows in his father's footsteps
- [ ] Two men with undershirts, one without
- [ ] A boy being tortured by a spider
- [ ] A show-off with sandcastles
- [ ] A gang of hat robbers
- [ ] An Arab making pyramids
- [ ] Three protruding tongues
- [ ] Two oddly fitting hats
- [ ] An odd couple
- [ ] Five sprinters
- [ ] A towel with a hole in it
- [ ] A cactus
- [ ] A boy who's not allowed any ice cream

## CAMP SITE
- [ ] A bull in a hedge
- [ ] Bull horns
- [ ] A shark in a canal
- [ ] A bull seeing red
- [ ] A careless kick
- [ ] Tea in a lap
- [ ] A low bridge
- [ ] People knocked over by a mallet
- [ ] A man surprised undressing
- [ ] A bicycle tire about to be punctured
- [ ] Camper's camels
- [ ] A scarecrow that doesn't work
- [ ] A wigwam
- [ ] Large biceps
- [ ] A collapsed tent
- [ ] A smoking barbecue
- [ ] A fisherman catching old boots
- [ ] Tacks on the path
- [ ] Boy scouts making fire
- [ ] A tired Santa
- [ ] A man blowing up a boat
- [ ] A camper's butler
- [ ] Runners on a road
- [ ] A bull chasing children
- [ ] Scruffy campers
- [ ] Thirsty walkers

## SPORTS STADIUM
- [ ] Three pairs of feet, sticking out of sand
- [ ] A cowboy starting races
- [ ] Hopeless hurdlers
- [ ] Ten children with fifteen legs
- [ ] A record thrower
- [ ] A shot-put juggler
- [ ] An ear trumpet
- [ ] A vaulting horse
- [ ] A runner with two wheels
- [ ] A parachuting vaulter
- [ ] A Scotsman with a caber
- [ ] An elephant pulling a rope
- [ ] People being knocked over by a hammer
- [ ] A gardener
- [ ] Three frogmen
- [ ] A naked runner
- [ ] A bed
- [ ] A bandaged boy
- [ ] A runner with four legs
- [ ] A sunken jumper
- [ ] A man with an odd pair of legs
- [ ] A man chasing a dog, chasing a cat
- [ ] A boy squirting water